10-04-2009

Gaylord and Grayjack

The Best of Friends

Gaylord and Grayjack

The Best of Friends

Mimi K.

Gaylord and Gray Jack
The Best of Friends

Printed in the United States of America

ISBN 978-1-935507-04-8

Cover Design & Page Layout by David Siglin of A&E Media

Illustrations copyright Virginia Petersen

Author Photograph by Lisa Clayton

AMBASSADOR INTERNATIONAL
Emerald House
427 Wade Hampton Blvd.
Greenville, SC 29609, USA
www.ambassador-international.com

AMBASSADOR PUBLICATIONS
Providence House
Ardenlee Street
Belfast, BT6 8QJ, Northern Ireland, UK
www.ambassador-productions.com

The colophon is a trademark of Ambassador

CPSIA compliance information: Batch # 293855BP

Visit Mimi at *www.mimikeenerbooks.com*

Acknowledgements

To Pam Poss, who was the first to encourage me to write this story some thirty years ago.

To my South Carolina friends, Linda Robertson, LaDonna Welch, Linda Garner, and Bonnie Foster, for faithfully listening and putting up with all my readings.

To David and Sherilyn Ammons, retired teachers, for teaching me better grammar and editing.

To the Keagle family, the Peter Johnson family for sharing the early beginnings of the book with their children. To the Dow Welsh family, Blair, Carter, Meredith and Holder for enjoying the adventures of Gaylord and Gray Jack.

To sweet little Reagan Moody for reading over the telephone "Chores of Fun" and laughing at all the right places.

To my Iowa friends, the Crill family, Christine, Clayton, Johnny, Sherry, and Mary for making life on the farm an adventure and making great suggestions.

To my beloved Sister, Ginny Petersen for illustrating this book and to my Brothers, Skippy and Bob for being good brothers and to my twin Brother, Michael, for being Gaylord and being Gray Jack's best friend.

About the Illustrator

Ginny Peterson resides in Salem, Oregon. She attended Nurses Training in Ottumwa, Iowa and graduated as a Register Nurse in 1957. She obtained her under grad from Stevens College, Columbia, MO., and her Masters degree from Kennedy University, Orinda, CA. Most of her professional career was spent in Health Care Administration serving over twenty three years with Kaiser Permanente, a large HMO in California. Ginny also grew up on the Rose Hill Farm and is the sister to Mimi K. At the age of 16 she discovered her artistic talents. It was short lived and she had to rediscover her artistry abilities again when she retired. She enjoys her three grandchildren, Andy, Steve, and Travis.

Prologue

In a time before computers, cell phones, Xbox and iPods, there lived a family of seven on a small farm outside of Rose Hill, Iowa. The Garrett family lived a simple life, filled with chores and animals. A family caring for the land, growing fruit trees and planting vegetable gardens.

It was 1951; Skippy, the oldest, had left home to join the Marines. Bob left home joining the Paratroopers. Virginia entered Nurses Training. The seven year old twins, Mike and Marion, were missing their brothers and sister.

Now it would be just the four of them, mom and dad, Marion and Michael. The twins had to learn to play on their own. It was a time to use their imaginations and figure out ways to fill their days! And fill them they did for the next six years with the adventures of their heroes, Gaylord and Gray Jack, The Best of Friends.

Table of Contents

A New Friend

On a steamy hot 4th of July, like a song at the river's edge, the Ferris wheel was a-turn'n and the cotton candy was a-stick'n everywhere. The town's people and the farmers were all a-mix'n and the carnies (the folks who worked at the carnival) were a-yell'n, "Come and win a chance to take home a stuffed animal!"

What Cheer! A small town located at the Skunk River's edge was never more alive than on the 4th of July. Every farmer and the local town's folks would bring their blankets and picnic baskets.

The Twins were eight years old and it was the first time they had been to a Fair. Both Mike and Marion ran all over the grounds taking in the site of a ferris wheel and the smell of hotdog stands. They could hardly wait to get a cold Root Beer Soda Pop and a scoop of home made ice cream.

Everywhere they looked there was food, cakes baked by the local farm women, corn on the cob, and cold watermelon. Then it happened. They spotted a large card board box and

FREE PUPPIES

peeking over the top was a furry little head with floppy black ears and barely hanging onto the inside edge of the box were two white paws. It was as if that creature could talk, "Help me, I am falling and cannot get out." The twins were immediately drawn to the box and the little fluffy creature! They had to help the black and white Australian Sheppard puppy out from his captivity.

Michael lifted him up and out of the box. Marion was squealing with joy at the sight of this puppy wagging its short black tail with a white tip at the end and seeing him licking at Michael's face.

"Let me hold him, let me hold him!" yelled Marion. So Michael handed him over to his twin sister. Marion and the puppy became instant friends.

It was mutual love at first sight and the twins knew they had found a new friend who would share their adventures. They asked the keeper of the puppy box to please save Snooky just for them.

They needed to get special permission from their parents. Rushing back to find their Mom and Dad, Carol and Doran, the twins, completely out of breath and barely able to speak finally uttered, "You have to meet our new friend, SNOOKY."

Life was never better than when SNOOKY joined the Garrett family. He went everywhere with the children, walking them to school he became known as the best educated dog in all of Delta County. This was before dog leashes. It was life on the farm, a time when folks trained and took care of their animals.

Snooky attended Burr Oak school every day with the twins, and during the day he would run through the fields hunting, always to return in time to walk home with the twins. Snooky never missed adventures with the twins for he was their friend.

The Jet and the Straw Hat

It all began after the twins had moved to the Rose Hill farm. Early one Saturday morning finishing up some of the morning chores Marion came up with an idea, "Why don't we give ourselves special names and become heroes when we go on adventures!"

Michael responded immediately to the idea, "I am going to be Gaylord, he is a great pilot".

"You can't take Gaylord, it's the name I wanted" shouted Marion.

"Well you can't have it, said Michael with gleaming eyes, "I got it first. You will have to come up with another name".

Gaylord was a close friend to the twins' older Brothers, Skip and Bob. He would often visit and sometimes wear his Air Force Pilot's uniform. One day the twins were sitting on a large rock watching their father ride on the old John Deer tractor. It was summer time and the sky was clear blue, not a cloud in sight.

To protect his face from the hot sun, the twins' dad wore a straw hat. Plowing the fields could take a full day and at the end of the day their dad was always shaking off the dust before supper time.

It must have been on that summer day Gaylord became the twins' hero. As they watched their dad plow the field, they noticed in the far distance three jets approaching and one was rather low. The low flying jet got closer and closer and then it came right over the top of their dad's head and the tractor. The jet's shadow covered the entire field. The belly of the plane was white with large deep blue letters painted on the side showing U.S.A. along with a big deep blue star. It was a colorful plane with a big red bull's eye around the front tip and big red tail.

The plane tipped its wings back and forth, waving at the twins as it passed over. The jet was so low that it looked like it caught the straw hat, knocking it into the air. At that moment the twins could not tell if that straw hat was flying above the jet. By this time their dad was standing up at the wheel of the tractor yelling something.

The twins could see his lips moving but could not make out what he was saying. As the dust settled they could see his long strong arm up in the air shaking a fist at the low flying jet. As their dad, Doran, slowly sat down he noticed that his so perfectly plowed field had a wild zigzag row! That night he was late for supper because he had a zigzag row to straighten out. The twins were rolling with laughter because they knew it was Gaylord having some fun with their dad.

This would be the last time the Jet would fly over the farm. It was the Korean War and Gaylord was called to fight for his country. Korea was far, far away from the Rose Hill, Iowa farm. The twin's mother told them it was located near China. Gaylord would never return from Korea. The twins were told that Gaylord flew to Korea and from Korea flew his jet right on up to Heaven to buzz the Wings of Angels. The twins figured that there were a lot of feathers floating around up there.

Marion was really upset with Michael and knew that she had to find a name

and hero to match Gaylord. It would take her a matter of minutes to make up her perfect hero. Her name would be Gray Jack. She was a fierce fighter for all underdogs and guardian of all that was good. She did not need a plane because she could fly without one.

Michael argued, "No one could fly without an airplane."

"Well Gray Jack can fly and you cannot have her name, she is my hero," Marion proudly answered.

From that moment on Gaylord and Gray Jack were the best of friends.

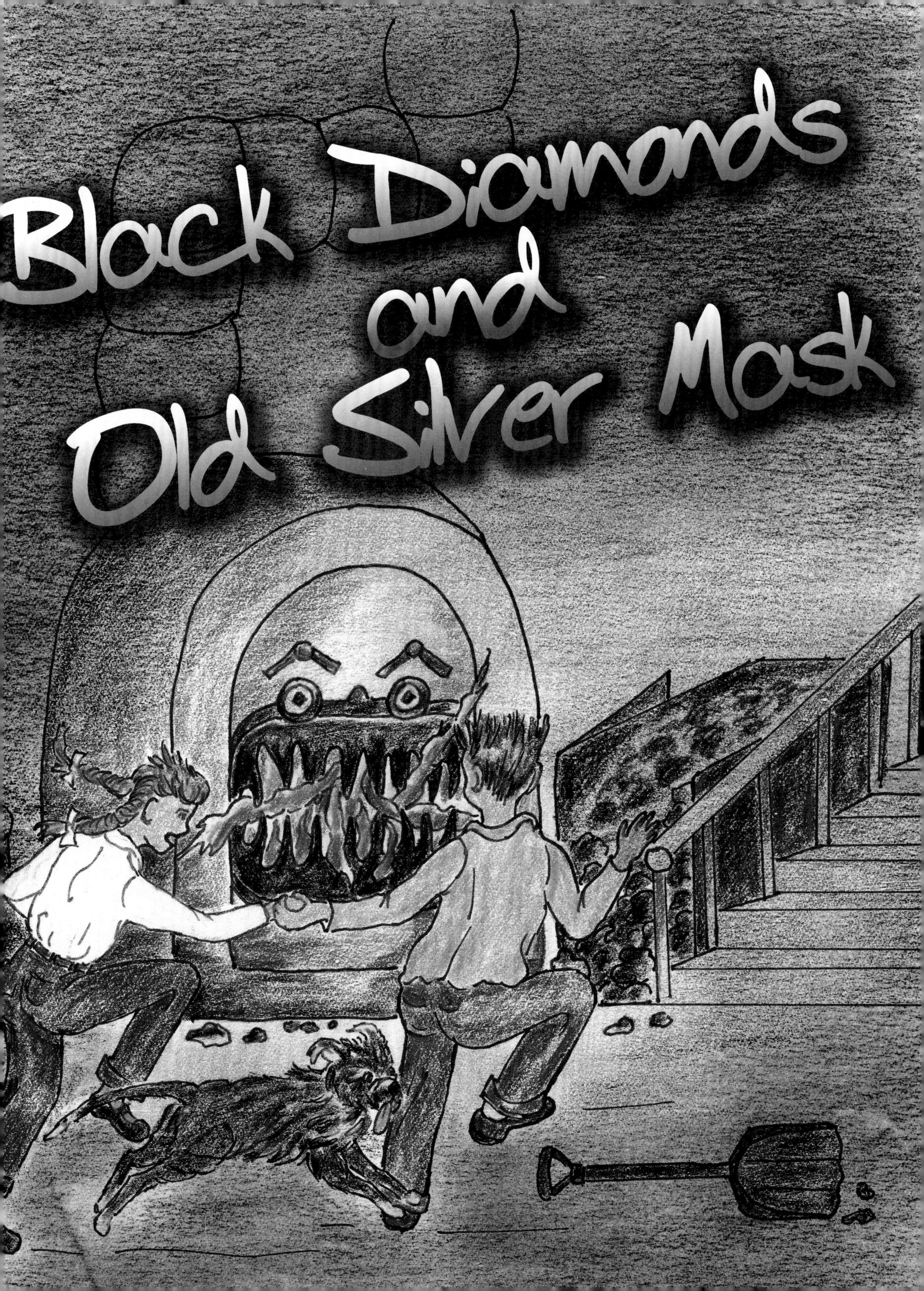
Black Diamonds
and
Old Silver Mask

Black Diamonds and Old Silver Mask

Gaylord and Gray Jack's adventures started when their mom and dad moved to a small farm outside of Rose Hill, Iowa. The two bedroom house had indoor plumbing and electricity. Having lights and running water was something totally new for the twins and a luxury for the Garrett family.

The twins had to share a bedroom and their room had two windows, one on each side of their bunk-beds. The windows had green shutters and when the wind would blow really fast, the shutters would swing back and forth making frightful sounds in the night.

The farm's small white barn sheltered the animals and held bales of hay. Near the barn stood the old corn crib and peeking through the cracks were the yellow ears of corn. The white chicken coop and fenced in chicken yard housed 100 chickens. Near the barn was a machine shed used to shelter a John Deer tractor.

The small farm house had a full basement where every winter Old Silver Mask, a monster, came out of hibernation to dominate the basement, his cave. The Twins were about to go into the cave and it was time to call upon Gaylord and Gray Jack, their secret names used when on dangerous missions.

The first winter on the Rose Hill Farm and all winters thereafter the twins would have to venture into Silver Mask's cave and look straight into the monster's mouth to see the roaring fire in his belly. The heat would take their breath away.

Their mother would ask the twins to go into the basement every night and put more coal on the fire. The black coal fueled the furnace giving heat necessary to warm the entire house. For the twins this meant a trip into the darkness of the basement to the coal bend where the Black Diamonds were stored near Old Silver Mask's cave. The Twins were sure that Old Silver Mask lived to see them as his last meal.

The twins would never go into the Black Diamond Mines alone; they had to protect one another from Silver Mask. Marion insisted that Mike go first and soon they were fighting over who would go first, "Gaylord would never be a coward" shouted Marion.

"So you are saying," responded Michael, "If I go first, Gray Jack is a coward?"

Marion thought a minute about what Michael had said and came up with a solution. "I did not say Gray Jack was a coward. Why don't we both go down the stairs at the same time on the same steps. Then we can be brave together."

They agreed and went down the stairs to the basement hand-in-hand, putting

their plan together step-by-step. By the time the explorers got to the bottom of the basement stairs they were ready to meet Old Silver Mask.

One would go into the Black Diamond Mines while the other watched for the basement demons, those little crystallized cinders, the sparks that leapt out of Old Silver Mask's mouth. These cinders would harden and purposely trip you. The last thing you wanted to see were the jaws of Old Silver Mask making you his next meal!

Gaylord would always be in charge of gathering the black diamonds, the food necessary to keep Old Silver Mask happy and up to the task of warming the entire house for the winter. Once the black diamonds filled the shovel, Gaylord immediately spoon fed the monster with three shovel loads of black diamonds. Lastly, Gaylord would release the latch that closed the monster's mouth.

It was always dark in the back of the basement where the monster lived. Even with a flashlight it was dark. Gaylord could come running out of there and right behind him Gray Jack was screaming, "Hurry! Hurry up!" Somehow during this time they always escaped just before the fire rose and Old Silver Mask's mouth closed.

Gaylord and Gray Jack would run as fast as they could towards the wooden steps leading them up and out of the basement. Always out of breath they arrived to the safety of the kitchen.

This routine took place every winter night before bedtime and Old Silver Mask would linger on in their dreams!

Come Home, It's Supper Time

The tree stood tall as it shaded the corridor, a hallway leading the cows from the pasture to the barn. The corridor became great travel through time for the adventurous twins. It was here they sailed the high seas, fought battles, and saved the farm from aliens.

The tree was their travel of choice. It allowed a platform to be built between two forked giant limbs. On board at the helm was an old rusted wagon wheel, set to turn on a post, guiding the ship through the sea pastures of the world.

As the season of high winds began, the wind lifted their ship up and down over the waves of grain and they knew they were in for the ride of their lives. On board they carried a brown bag of rations which included a peanut butter and jelly sandwich, an orange, a large glass jar of water and in case they got shipped wrecked, two large jaw breakers. The jaw breakers could last for days!

No ship was complete without a dog, and getting Snooky on board was no small challenge, but the ever enterprising twins made up a pulley with rope and lifted the ship's guard dog on board. Gaylord would be on deck calling down to Gray Jack, "Lift Snooky up when I count to three and I will pull as you push."

"Ok I got him. Start counting and hurry. He is heavy" cried Gray Jack.

Gaylord began pulling as hard as he could and Gray Jack pushed as hard as she could and finally Snooky was on board. As the wind blew the ship began to sway back and forth. The howls of delight from both crew and dog could be heard all over the world.

From sun-up to sun-down the ship carried the three from the farm to the far reaches of the world. As it came back to the corridor and docked, the three passengers in adventure headed back to the farm house lured by the aroma of homemade baked bread. They could hear their mother's sweet voice calling, "Come home, it's supper time."

Burr Oak Table of Torture

On early sunlit mornings, with Snooky at their side, the twins walked through their field of dreams. Climbing wooden fences, hopping over small creeks, avoiding cow pies, and counting the many stalks of corn, the twins would arrive at school.

In the early 1950's some one room school houses dotted the edges of corn fields in Iowa, providing rural children formal educations. Burr Oak was no stranger to 13 children who resided on surrounding farms. The Crills, the Kuntz's, the White family and the Garrett twins, Mike and Marion, the only twins in Rose Hill, would walk to school each day along with Snooky to meet up with their friends, Johnny, Sherry, and Mary. The Crills always rode in on their ponies, Billy and Fudge.

Michael and Marion loved having play time with the Crills, and on a few Saturdays they were allowed to go to the Crill Farm, where everyone got to saddle up their own horse and the adventures of Cowboy and Indians began. The boys would always challenge the girls and the game was hide-'n seek on horse back. The Girls would head out first and always outwitted the boys. Play time with other children took place mostly between the outings on the Crill Farm and Burr Oak.

It was amazing how everyone was able to learn the three R's, "reading, writing, and arithmetic" with no air conditioning, no running water and no indoor plumbing. At the front of the classroom, surrounded by 13 small desks, stood the old oil burning stove. To the left side of the stove was a child size wooden table with four children's chairs. One slightly larger chair for Mrs. Deweese, respectfully addressed as "TEACHER".

TEACHER was slight in size and always wore the same outfit, a white sleeveless cotton blouse and a homemade black cotton skirt gathered at the waistband and held by one single button. She donned her feet with black ballerina like shoes and never wore stockings until wintertime when she choose to wrap her feet in white cotton socks. She also had a big black button-down sweater for winter. Mrs. Deweese was constant every day in every way. She made sure that all 13 children were learning and did not miss a step with their education.

Each day TEACHER would start with the salute to the flag, then proceed to have each grade level come up front to sit at the "Table", better known to the children as, "The Table of Torture".

Right after lunch and recess she would bring the children in and have everyone rest their heads on the desk as she read from the book (Angel Unaware) written by their first television heroes, Roy Rogers and Dale Evans. This

was a 30 minute tradition and a favorite time to hear Teacher's voice expressing thoughts from books. As she finished, the children knew what was waiting for them. It was back to the "Table of Torture" the table where Michael and Marion had to read out loud, or do their additions and subtractions.

The "Table of Torture" was keeping two children from exploring the world. The twins longed to be outdoors on adventures with Snooky. The table exposed their reading disabilities.

The "Table of Torture" was where two children had to learn how to read and write. The table where a teacher took time to teach 13 special children. The table where TEACHER loved seeing the twins learn. Eventually Teacher and the "Table of Torture" took away the fear of reading and writing.

She gave the greatest gift to the twins. She taught them how to read without fear and her dedication opened up brand new worlds of adventure for Gaylord and Gray Jack!

Chores of Fun

Being on a farm required the entire family's participation. Everyone had responsibilities and the twins must be dependable in every aspect of their assigned chores. There were some things only grown ups were allowed to do… milking the cows, feeding the hogs, plowing the fields, and cutting the oats. Because they were only eight years old, the twins were tasked with feeding the 100 chickens. Their duties would include gathering eggs, bringing up the cows from the pasture and feeding them. The twins had to be up early each morning to feed the chickens. The rest of the chores would take place around 4:00 p.m. every afternoon. This was the routine their Father, Doran, expected the twins to follow.

Chickens can be very boring, and gathering eggs sometimes very messy. Before entering the coop, Marion would put on a pair of boots and gloves. Hoping not to get pecked, Marion would carefully put her hand in the nest under the sitting chicken and pull out the chicken's eggs.

The coops were cleaned every other day by replacing the old nests with fresh yellow straw. Michael washed the cement floors using a bucket of water and mop. Then he would wait for the floor to dry and place fresh yellow straw from one end of the coop to the other. Anywhere those chickens spent any length of time, they had a bad habit of disposing of their body waste, leaving the nests and coup floors full of chicken "do-do".

Marion would always gather the eggs and place them into a special wire bucket. Then she headed to the house where she would wash each egg and place it in a clean wire basket. Once she completed this task, she would keep out enough eggs to feed the family for that day. Doran would take the eggs into town and sell them to the Country Store.

One afternoon while Marion was cleaning the eggs she glanced out the kitchen window to see an amazing sight in the chicken yard. There were at least 70 chickens lying on their backs with their yellow claw feet and beaks sticking straight up in the air. She ran outside to get a closer look and behold there was Michael with a smirk on his face, holding a chicken in his one hand and pointing his finger right between the chicken's eyes.

In a second the chicken was hypnotized and flat on its back. His goal was to get all 100 chickens knocked out for a few minutes right before their dad arrived, so he would think they had all croaked.

As their dad drove up the drive all he could see were 100 chickens lying dead on their backs in the chicken yard. Barely able to keep from bursting out with laughter, Michael and Marion hid behind the old John Deer tractor. The chickens began to come to life one by one. On that day the twins found out that their father did not   have a good sense of humor, at least in front of them. Needless to   say, it was the last time that the "Chores of Fun" occurred and   Michael never performed the "Croaked Chicken Act" again!

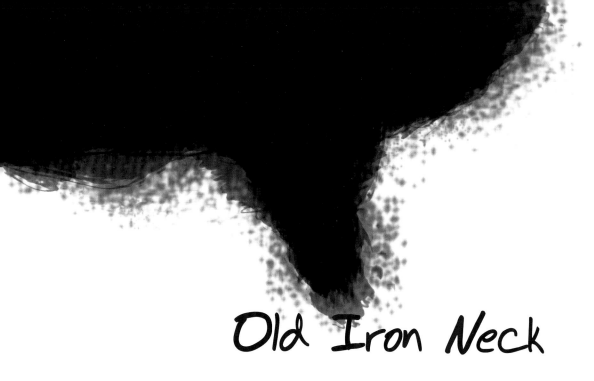

Old Iron Neck

It was Saturday, and with early morning chores completed, the twins ventured out to save the world before supper time. With Snooky at their side they were ready to conquer Iron Neck the monster that lived down in the clay caves located five fields and one river away from the Garrett Farm. Mike and Marion would again become Gaylord and Gray Jack, the "Indiana Jones" of Rose Hill, Iowa. These two explorers would cross the Nile River, known to the locals as the Skunk River. Here they would board their makeshift raft, place their days rations which included a peanut butter and jelly sandwich, one jar of water, and just in-case they were stranded for any length of time, the addition of two jawbreakers.

Snooky loved water and most of the time ended up swimming behind the raft. When he got tired, the twins would get close to shore and let him jump on board. Their journey today would take them to the land of Old Iron Neck where they would sneak about to check out the damage made by the monster's giant jaws.

This day was no ordinary day, for as they approached the clay caves, they could not hear the monster's mighty jaws eating the earth. For a moment the twins were alarmed that old Iron Neck had heard them approaching and was lying in wait for them. They grabbed Snooky and looked around and about to make sure they were safe. Then very slowly approaching the clay grave yard, the home of Old Iron Neck, they spotted him. There he lay, his neck and jaws spread out on the ground, just peacefully sleeping. Gaylord and Gray Jack for the first time could actually get a closer look with the possibility of touching Old Iron Neck. Gaylord was the first to venture down into the home pit and then he did something most daring. He climbed onto the monster's giant neck then right into his Jaws. It did not disturb the monster, so followed Gray Jack, and then Snooky, all three having the time of their lives crawling around and about on Iron Neck.

They had never seen the monster sleep before. He was always chewing up the earth and spitting it back out. He was ruining the beautiful pasture area and chewing up the trees. When he was awake, his iron neck stood 50 feet tall and his jaws could pick up a whole car. He polluted the quiet countryside with a cranky loud noise and billowing smoke and could be heard as far away as downtown Rose Hill, a town of one board walk, one post office, one church, one bar, and 20 homes. It was truly a country town.

Adventure in time has a way of passing by quickly. From a far distance they could hear the farm bell ringing and the twins knew that they had to get out of the monster's jaws before he heard the bell and awoke. They did not want to be Old Iron Neck's dinner. The farm bell let them know that Carol, their mother, was looking for them. It was time to get back to the raft, eat their rations, and head home.

Dots of Love

As the days went by on the farm, the twins loved walking through the fields to Burr Oak, and always looked forward to playing at school with the other children. It was the only time they had a chance to be with people. On their way they would be climbing fences, running from the bulls, jumping over creeks, and watching for wild rabbits. Coming home after school, with Snooky by their sides, they would take the dirt road on dry days and at the halfway mark, the gravel road. The gravel trucks and graders would put big piles of gravel on each side of the road and the twins would make believe they were skating through the piles. It was about five miles of walking every day which gave the twins time to think of those things that would help Gaylord and Gray Jack be better equipped for their world adventures.

The twins had made slingshots out of sturdy twigs, but now they needed something that could put a monster to sleep. It had to be monster proof and magically make the monster experience goodness, kindness, and acceptance of others. Their mother had always told them to practice the "Golden Rule"... To do unto others as you would have them do unto you. They wanted the monster to learn this rule.

So they thought about this for several days making lists of things that made them happy. They loved listening to the radio, "The Shadow Knows", "The

Lone Ranger", and "Amos and Andy", but they couldn't carry the big old radio with them. Besides, they did not have electricity on their ship. Cheerios for breakfast always made them happy, but their mother would not let them bag up valuable food.

They loved looking at the old Sears catalog. It always made them sleepy and filled their dreams with lots of magical pictures-pictures of things they had never seen before. That was it, the catalog was the answer. It could put anyone to sleep and make them see the brighter side of life. Mike came up with the blow dart idea and Marion came up with the magic of little round dots.

Between the two creative geniuses they came up with recycling last years catalog. They would take the least interesting section (appliances) roll four pages together to make a strong tube, and then tape the edges with Scotch tape. The next step was to find the most colorful parts of the catalog (usually clothing) and use a hole punch to make the ammunition of love. It was perfect. Now it was time to make up their lists of things they needed:

1. Two old catalogs
2. Pages of colorful pictures
3. 1 pair of scissors
4. 1 roll of scotch tape
5. 1 hole punch
6. 2 brown paper bags
7. Twine rope from the barn

For the next few Sundays they worked each afternoon punching out the dots. After loading the dots into two brown paper bags the twins tied the top of each bag with the twine.

Gaylord and Gray Jack were ready for the next adventure. They had their blow guns loaded with the ammunition of colorful dots. They were ready to shower any monster they meant with their dots of love, teaching those monsters what the "GOLDEN RULE" really meant. Their mother had always told them that the Golden Rule taught us to "Do unto others as we would have them do unto us". So the twins figured if they shot their dots of the love at any monsters they encountered, the monsters in life would surely appreciate learning about loving one another!

Sunday Surprise

Sunday Surprise

The twin's Mother, Carol, would always whip up pancakes, scrambled eggs, and bacon, making Sunday mornings exciting at the Garrett house. After breakfast the twins would get ready for God's time. Their mother would say, "This is the day to worship the God of Abraham when the world stops and rests." Sunday was a time when all businesses would be closed.

The twins loved Sunday. It was the day to wear their church shoes and Sunday school clothes. Their mother told them, "You should always look your very best when you go to God's house of worship." So on Saturday nights the twins got a full bath, with heads washed. Marion got to put curlers in her hair. She always wore braids during the week, and on Sundays she wore her long curly hair loose.

Carol made all the twin's clothes, except for their jeans; she bought those from the town store. In order to make up the shirts for Michael and dresses for Marion, their mother would save the cotton fabric from the flour sacks.

In the 1950's through the 1960's girls were required to wear dresses. This was very stressful for Marion, as she had to wear a dress every day to Burr Oak School. When it was cold she had to wear snow pants under her dress.

She wondered, "Why?"

"It is just the way it is," replied her mother, "Girls are to be girls and boys are to be boys."

Marion somehow knew, in her heart, that pants would not make her any less a girl. She got to wear pants after school and it did not change her into a boy; however, she did conclude that boys would really look funny in dresses and somehow that could affect them for life. She concluded that Michael would not be caught dead in a dress.

This Sunday would be full of surprises for the twins. Their mother taught Sunday school and also played the piano for the Rose Hill Community Church and on this Sunday she was also singing a song, "For the Beauty of the Earth."

Carol was always hurrying around on Sunday mornings while their Dad, Doran, relaxed and read the local newspaper. Michael and Marion's favorite part of the newspaper was the cartoon section. Doran would attend church only on Easter and Christmas, so this particular morning he missed hearing Carol sing!

It was in Sunday school that Gaylord and Gray Jack learned about David and Goliath, and how David slew the giant with a slingshot and one stone. It was after this lesson that the slingshot became Gaylord and Gray Jack's choice of defense.

Sunday school had ended and it was time for Big People's Church. The Twins always had to sit on the front pew nearest the piano so Carol could keep a close eye on them. Michael would always get himself into trouble by getting Marion to laugh or giggle. Their attention span was about as long as a moment in time.

The twins tried to be good, but the lack of focus would always get them into trouble with the exception of this Sunday morning. Something happened that changed their lives.

There he was, a giant of a man, sitting on the church platform, Marion and Michael were startled by what they saw. This man had the most beautiful smile and was the color of dark chocolate. He saw the twins and knew by their innocent expressions that they had never seen a black man before. Neither moved, their eyes were glued on him. When he stood up he was even taller and his hands were so large they could hold a dozen eggs.

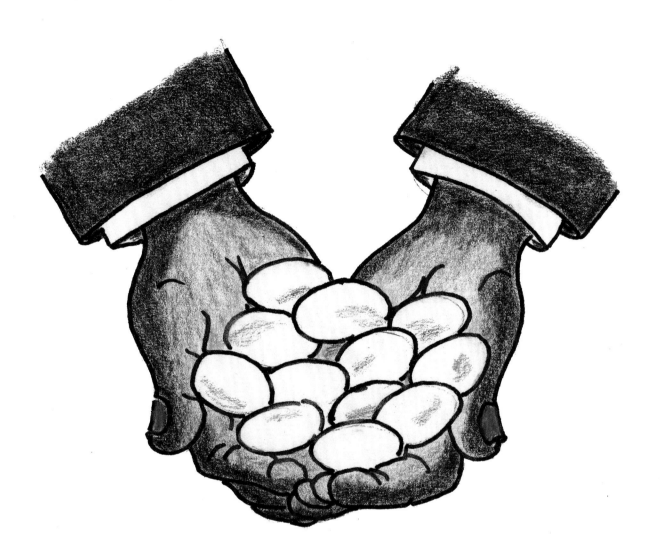

When he opened his mouth to sing, inside was the most beautiful pink. The palms of his hands were even a deeper pink. His big eyes glistened and his teeth were perfect pearls. The two listened to every word this missionary from Africa had to say. He spoke the English language differently, but the twins understood every word.

His story told about Jesus and how he came to know Jesus personally. This was good news. Not only did they see this extraordinary man, but now they knew someone who actually knew Jesus. What a day this was for them. They had only known Jesus through books and stories and now they were about to meet someone who had actually met Him!

Carol knew that the Twins were taken with this missionary's Message and totally absorbed with his color. Carol and Doran had never used bad words or spoken poorly of any other race. The Twins only saw and heard from a great man. If he were a friend of Jesus, he was a friend of theirs.

After the service, Carol brought the twins up to meet the Great Chocolate Man. Marion said to him, "Please smile and let me see the palms of your hands." She held his hands telling him,"

"You are the most beautiful person I have ever seen, I love your colors."

Carol immediately followed the comment, "Please understand that you are the first black person the children have ever seen."

He broke out in laughter and hugged the awestruck twins telling them, "Jesus loves all the little children of the world."

When the twins got home they immediately went to their globe to find Africa and look for the place where their new friend lived. It was on that Sunday that Carol sat the twins down and explained how many different races and colors there were in the world and that everyone belonged to the family of God.

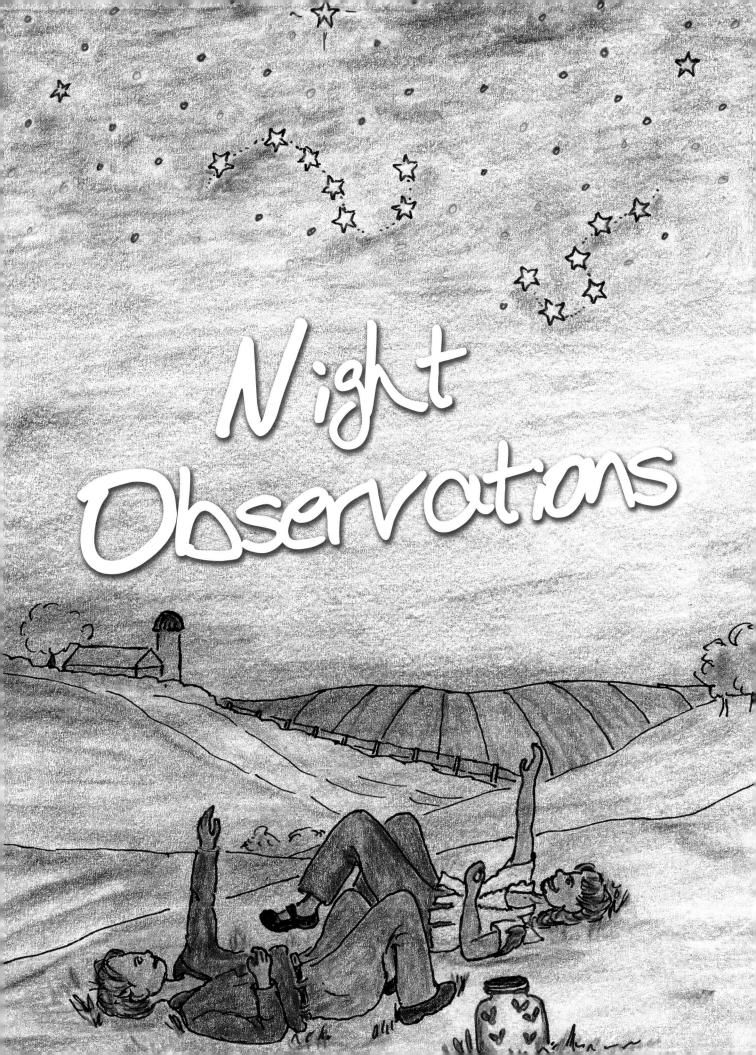

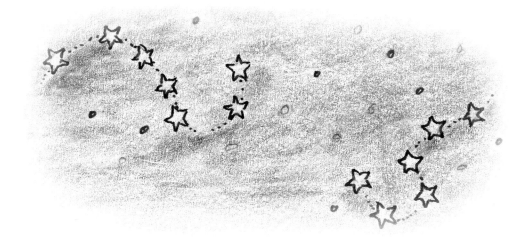

Night Observations

In the summer time after the evening chores and dinner, the twins would spend time sitting on the kitchen porch watching Snooky chase lighting bugs. They joined in the fun with their jars trying to catch a few! After a while falling to the ground with exhaustion, they would lie on their backs in the freshly cut green grass and gaze at the night sky.

It was as though the sky had its very own lighting bugs, with some of them plunging to earth. It was always a ritual for the twins to wash their feet before bed time. Carol, their mother, would have a large tin wash basin big enough for them to both wash up at the same time. Then they would go into the house and wash their hands and face and brush their teeth.

Once they had completed their personal chores, Carol would join with them for a special time of prayer. She would always have them pray for the family, children of the world, and to thank the Lord for blessings.

The twins slept in a small bedroom with wooden bunk beds. The favorite place to sleep for Marion was always on the top bunk. With Mike below pushing with both feet right into the springs of that upper bunk she would expect to have the ride of her life up there! Marion would hold on for dear life or go flying out of the bed. Soon they would hear their father telling them to settle down.

It was difficult to close their eyes as they would catch the moonlight shadows dancing on the walls and ceiling of their bedroom.

"Michael, Michael," whispered Marion, Did you see that?"

"See what" questioned Michael?

Marion quickly responded, "Something moved on the far wall. Now, it is moving toward you."

Pulling himself back as far as he could in his lower bunk, Michael in a weak whisper asked, "Where, which wall, how close is it?"

"It is now below your bunk, ready to crawl up the bed post and it is looking for you" answered Marion.

With panic in his whisper, "What should I do," asked Michael?

Marion, with a giggle, whispered back, "I would suggest you get out of there and go pull the window shade and get rid of that moonlight shadow about to attack you!"

At that moment Michael put his feet to the top of his bunk and pushed the upper bunk so hard that Marion went flying out of bed and landed on the floor with a loud thump!

They could hear their dad coming down the hall and this could not be good.

"Ok kids, I am not going to tell you again to settle down. The next time I come in there you both will be in deep trouble."

The twins knew their dad meant what he said and they immediately settled down. The evening had come to an end. Pulling the covers up over their heads they soon closed their eyes to dream of more adventures with Gaylord and Gray Jack.

Johnny, Mary, and Sherry Crill riding 'Billy'.

Sherry riding 'Fudge'.

(School) Burr Oak Country School (1953)

The Rose Hill farm house (1951)

The Rose Hill farm house (1995)

Summer Surprises!

Adventures of Gaylord and Grayjack (1951-1957)

By Mimi K.

Several years have past since the twins moved to the Rose Hill farm. They had explored most of the area surrounding the farm including the Clay Pits.

Snooky had joined them when he was a puppy and now he was a full grown dog. The twins were already looking forward to the summer of 1956.

In the winter they had to deal with Old Silver Mask and both knew if they made it to March they had escaped the Black Diamond Mines and the jaws of Old Silver Mask. They also would be free from the Table of Torture for at least three months. How they longed to be outdoors exploring the world they knew so well, those wonderful fields and rivers of Rose Hill.

This summer would bring many surprises for the twins, surprises beyond their imaginations, surprises beyond the reaches of the farm, beyond the reaches of the Rose Hill and Watch Cheer. This would be the Summer of Surprises!

Summer Surprises! includes:

Canaries and Cakes

Old Spider Hand

Fire, Fire

Music in the Corn Field

The Georgia Peach and Coca Cola

Kitchen Talk and Dusty Fields

The Marine and Ice Cream

Run and Hide

Visitors from a Distant Land

Keep up to date at www.mimikeenerbooks.com